D1505512

177
Favorite Poems
for Children

Wynken, Blynken, and Nod

177
Favorite Poems
for Children

Edited by Patricia Horan

Illustrated by Marilyn Weber

Avenel Books

A Division of Crown Publishers, Inc., New York

This book is especially for Meghan,
born, as is all poetry,
of patience, faith
and
a very small idea.

Copyright © MCMLXXIV by Crown Publishers, Inc.
Library of Congress Catalog Card Number: 74-77813
All rights reserved.
This edition is published by Avenel Books
a division of Crown Publishers, Inc.
a   b   c   d   e   f   g   h
Manufactured in the United States of America

Book designed by Carol Callaway

Contents

PEOPLE WHO USED TO BE

SMALL WORLD

JUST FOR LAUGHS

WISE WORDS

SONGS WITHOUT MUSIC

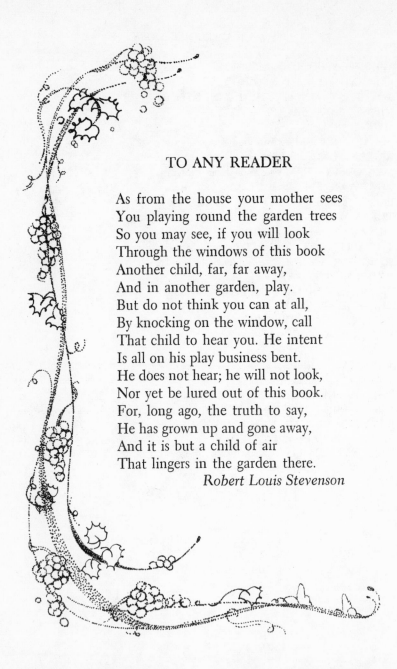

TO ANY READER

As from the house your mother sees
You playing round the garden trees
So you may see, if you will look
Through the windows of this book
Another child, far, far away,
And in another garden, play.
But do not think you can at all,
By knocking on the window, call
That child to hear you. He intent
Is all on his play business bent.
He does not hear; he will not look,
Nor yet be lured out of this book.
For, long ago, the truth to say,
He has grown up and gone away,
And it is but a child of air
That lingers in the garden there.

Robert Louis Stevenson

People Who Never Were

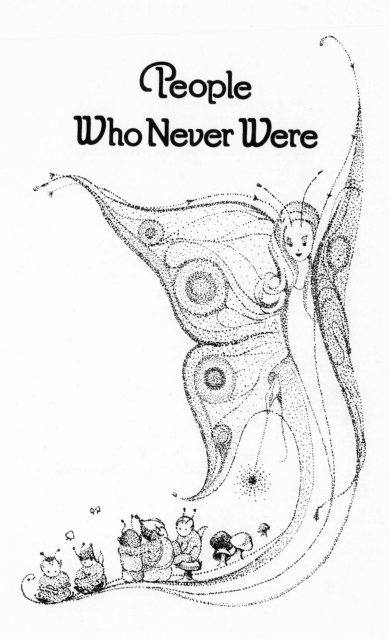

LITTLE BILLEE

There were three sailors of Bristol city
Who took a boat and went to sea.
But first with beef and captain's biscuits
And pickled pork they loaded she.

There was gorging Jack and guzzling Jimmy,
And the youngest he was little Billee.
Now when they got as far as the Equator
They'd nothing left but one split pea.

Says gorging Jack to guzzling Jimmy,
'I am extremely hungaree.'
To gorging Jack says guzzling Jimmy,
'We've nothing left, us must eat we.'

Says gorging Jack to guzzling Jimmy,
'With one another we shouldn't agree!
There's little Bill, he's young and tender,
We're old and tough, so let's eat he'.

'Oh! Billy, we're going to kill and eat you,
So undo the button of your chemie.'
When Bill received this information
He used his pocket handkerchie.

'First let me say my catechism,
Which my poor mammy taught to me.'
'Make haste, make haste,' says guzzling Jimmy,
While Jack pulled out his snickersnee.

So Billy went up to the main-top gallant mast,
And down he fell on his bended knee.
He scarce had come to the twelfth commandment
When up he jumps, 'There's land I see:

'Jerusalem and Madagascar,
And North and South Amerikee:
There's the British flag a-riding at anchor,
With Admiral Napier, K.C.B.'

So when they got aboard of the Admiral's,
He hanged fat Jack and flogged Jimmee;
But as for little Bill he made him
The Captain of a Seventy-three.

William Makepeace Thackeray

O CAPTAIN! MY CAPTAIN!

O Captain! My Captain! our fearful trip is done,
The ship has weather'd every rack, the prize we sought is won,
The port is near, the bells I hear, the people all exulting,
While fellow eyes the steady keel, the vessel grim and daring;
   But O Heart! heart! heart!
    O the bleeding drops of red,
      Where on the deck my Captain lies,
        Fallen cold and dead.

O Captain! my Captain! rise up and hear the bells;
Rise up—for you the flag is flung—for you the bugle trills,
For you bouquets and ribbon'd wreaths—for you the shores
   a-crowding,
For you they call, the swaying mass, their eager faces turning;
   Here Captain! dear father!
    This arm beneath your head!
      It is some dream that on the deck,
        You've fallen cold and dead.

My Captain does not answer, his lips are pale and still,
My father does not feel my arm, he has no pulse nor will,
The ship is anchor'd safe and sound, its voyage closed and
    done,
From fearful trip the victor ship comes in with object won;
  Exult O shores, and ring O bells!
    But I with mournful tread,
      Walk the deck my Captain lies,
        Fallen cold and dead.

Walt Whitman

THERE WAS A NAUGHTY BOY

There was a naughty boy
And a naughty boy was he.
He ran away to Scotland,
The people for to see.
  But he found
  That the ground
  Was as hard,
  That a yard
  Was as long,
  That a song
  Was as merry,
  That a cherry
  Was as red,
  That lead
  Was as weighty,
  That fourscore
  Was still eighty,
  And a door was as wooden as in England.
So he stood in his shoes and he wondered,
He wondered, he wondered,
So he stood in his shoes and he wondered.

John Keats

EXCELSIOR

The shades of night were falling fast,
As though an Alpine village passed
A youth who bore, 'mid snow and ice,
A banner with a strange device,
    Excelsior!

His brow was sad; his eyes beneath,
Flashed like a falchion from its sheath,
And like a silver clarion rung
The accents of that unknown tongue,
    Excelsior!

In happy homes he saw the light
Of household fires gleam warm and bright;
Above, the spectral glaciers shone,
And from his lips escaped a groan,
    Excelsior!

"Try not the Pass!" the old man said;
"Dark lowers the tempest overhead,
The roaring torrent is deep and wide!"
And loud that clarion voice replied,
    Excelsior!

"Oh stay," the maiden said, "and rest
Thy weary head upon this breast!"
A tear stood in his bright blue eye,
But still he answered, with a sigh,
    Excelsior!

"Beware the pine-tree's withered branch!
Beware the awful avalanche!"
This was the peasant's last Good-night,
A voice replied, far up the height,
    Excelsior!

At break of day, as heavenward
The pious monks of Saint Bernard
Uttered the oft-repeated prayer,
A voice cried through the startled air,
                    Excelsior!

A traveler, by the faithful hound,
Half buried in the snow was found,
Still grasping in his hand of ice
That banner with the strange device,
                    Excelsior!

There in the twilight cold and gray,
Lifeless, but beautiful, he lay,
And from the sky, serene and far,
A voice fell, like a falling star,
                    Excelsior!
                    Henry Wadsworth Longfellow

THE MODERN HIAWATHA

He killed the noble Mudjokivis,
With the skin he made him mittens,
Made them with the fur side inside,
Made them with the skin side outside,
He, to get the warm side inside,
Put the inside skin side outside:
He, to get the cold side outside,
Put the warm side fur side inside:
That's why he put the fur side inside,
Why he put the skin side outside,
Why he turned them inside outside.
                    George A. Strong

THE SOLITARY REAPER

Behold her, single in the field,
Yon solitary Highland Lass!
Reaping and singing by herself;
Stop here, or gently pass!
Alone she cuts and binds the grain,
And Sings a melancholy strain;
O listen! for the Vale profound
Is overflowing with the sound.

No Nightingale did ever chant
More welcome notes to weary bands
Of travellers in some shady haunt,
Among Arabian sands:
A voice so thrilling ne'er was heard
In spring-time from the Cuckoo-bird.
Breaking the silence of the seas
Among the farthest Hebrides.

Will no one tell me what she sings?—
Perhaps the plaintive numbers flow
For old, unhappy, far-off things,
And battles long ago:
Or, is it some more humble lay,
Familiar matter of to-day?
Some natural sorrow, loss, or pain,
That has been, and may be again?

Whate'er the theme, the Maiden sang
As if her song could have no ending;
I saw her singing at her work,
And o'er the sickle bending;—
I listened, motionless and still;
And, as I mounted up the hill,

The music in my heart I bore,
Long after it was heard no more.
William Wordsworth

THE OWL AND THE PUSSY-CAT

The Owl and the Pussy-cat went to sea
    In a beautiful pea-green boat,
They took some honey, and plenty of money,
    Wrapped up in a five-pound note.
The Owl looked up to the stars above,
    And sang to a small guitar,
'O lovely Pussy! O Pussy, my love,
    What a beautiful Pussy you are,
        You are,
        You are!
    What a beautiful Pussy you are!'

Pussy said to the Owl, 'You elegant fowl!
    How charmingly sweet you sing!
O let us be married! too long we have tarried:
    But what shall we do for a ring?'
They sailed away, for a year and a day,
    To the land where the Bong-tree grows
And there in a wood a Piggy-wig stood
    With a ring at the end of his nose,
        His nose,
        His nose,
    With a ring at the end of his nose.

'Dear Pig, are you willing to sell for one shilling
    Your ring?' Said the Piggy, 'I will.'

So they took it away, and were married next day
   By the Turkey who lives on the hill.
They dined on mince, and slices of quince,
   Which they ate with a runcible spoon;
And hand in hand, on the edge of the sand,
   They danced by the light of the moon,
      The moon,
      The moon,
   They danced by the light of the moon.

Edward Lear

MR. NOBODY

I know a funny little man,
   As quiet as a mouse,
Who does the mischief that is done
   In everybody's house!
There's no one ever sees his face,
   And yet we all agree
That every plate we break was cracked
   By Mr. Nobody.

'Tis he who always tears our books,
   Who leaves the door ajar,
He pulls the buttons from our shirts,
   And scatters pins afar;
That squeaking door will always squeak,
   For, prithee, don't you see,
We leave the oiling to be done
   By Mr. Nobody.

He puts damp wood upon the fire,
   That kettles cannot boil;
His are the feet that bring in mud,

And all the carpets soil.
The papers always are mislaid,
 Who had them last but he?
There's no one tosses them about
 But Mr. Nobody.

The finger-marks upon the door
 By none of us are made;
We never leave the blinds unclosed,
 To let the curtains fade.
The ink we never spill; the boots
 That lying round you see
Are not our boots;—they all belong
 To Mr. Nobody.

Anonymous

From THE JUMBLIES

They went to sea in a Sieve, they did,
 In a Sieve they went to sea:
In spite of all their friends could say,
On a winter's morn, on a stormy day,
 In a Sieve they went to sea!
And when the Sieve turned round and round,
And everyone cried, "You'll all be drowned!"
They called aloud, "Our Sieve ain't big,
But we don't care a button! we don't care a fig!

In a Sieve we'll go to sea!"
 Far and few, far and few,
 Are the lands where the Jumblies live;
 Their heads are green, and their hands are blue,
 And they went to sea in a Sieve.

Edward Lear

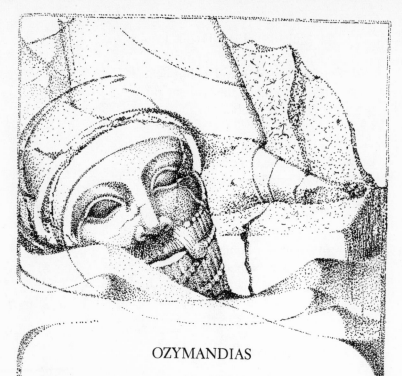

OZYMANDIAS

I met a traveller from an antique land
Who said: Two vast and trunkless legs of stone
Stand in the desert. . . . Near them, on the sand,
Half sunk, a shattered visage lies, whose frown,
And wrinkled lip, and sneer of cold command,
Tell that its sculptor well those passions read
Which yet survive, stamped on these lifeless things,
The hand that mocked them, and the heart that fed:
And on the pedestal these words appear:
'My name is Ozymandias, king of kings:
Look on my works, ye Mighty, and despair!'
Nothing beside remains. Round the decay
Of that colossal wreck, boundless and bare
The lone and level sands stretch far away.

P. B. Shelley

THE DUEL

The gingham dog and the calico cat
Side by side on the table sat;
'Twas half-past twelve, and (what do you think!)
Nor one nor t'other had slept a wink!
   The old Dutch clock and the Chinese plate
   Appeared to know as sure as fate
There was going to be a terrible spat.
      (*I wasn't there; I simply state*
      What was told to me by the Chinese plate!)

The gingham dog went "bow-wow-wow!"
And the calico cat replied "mee-ow!"
The air was littered, an hour or so,
With bits of gingham and calico,
   While the old Dutch clock in the chimney-place
   Up with its hands before its face,
For it always dreaded a family row!
      (*Now mind: I'm only telling you*
      What the old Dutch clock declares is true!)

The Chinese plate looked very blue,
And wailed, "Oh, dear! what shall we do!"
But the gingham dog and the calico cat
Wallowed this way and tumbled that,
Employing every tooth and claw
In the awfullest way you ever saw—
And, oh! how the gingham and calico flew!
      (*Don't fancy I exaggerate—*
      I got my news from the Chinese plate!)

Next morning, where the two had sat
They found no trace of dog or cat;
And some folks think unto this day

That burglars stole that pair away!
  But the truth about the cat and pup
  Is this: they ate each other up!
Now what do you really think of that!
    (*The old Dutch clock it told me so,*
    And that is how I came to know.)

Eugene Field

LITTLE BOY BLUE

The little toy dog is covered with dust,
  But sturdy and staunch he stands;
And the little toy soldier is red with rust,
  And his musket moulds in his hands.
Time was when the little toy dog was new,
  And the soldier was passing fair;
And that was the time when our Little Boy Blue
  Kissed them and put them there.

"Now, don't you go till I come," he said,
  "And don't you make any noise!"
So, toddling off to his trundle-bed,
  He dreamt of the pretty toys;
And, as he was dreaming, an angel song
  Awakened our Little Boy Blue—
Oh! the years are many, the years are long,
  But the little toy friends are true!

Aye, faithful to Little Boy Blue they stand,
  Each in the same old place—
Awaiting the touch of a little hand,
  The smile of a little face;

And they wonder, as waiting the long years through
    In the dust of that little chair,
What has become of our Little Boy Blue,
    Since he kissed them and put them there.

                              Eugene Field

FATHER WILLIAM

"You are old, Father William," the young man said,
    "And your hair has become very white;
And yet you incessantly stand on your head—
    Do you think, at your age, it is right?"

"In my youth," Father William replied to his son,
    "I feared it might injure the brain;
But now that I'm perfectly sure I have none,
    Why, I do it again and again."

"You are old," said the youth, "as I mentioned before,
    And have grown most uncommonly fat;
Yet you turned a back-somersault in at the door—
    Pray, what is the reason of that?"

"In my youth," said the sage, as he shook his gray locks,
    "I kept all my limbs very supple
By the use of this ointment—one shilling the box—
    Allow me to sell you a couple?"

"You are old," said the youth, "and your jaws are too weak
    For anything tougher than suet;
Yet you finished the goose, with the bones and the beak—
    Pray, how did you manage to do it?"

"In my youth," said his father, "I took to the law,
    And argued each case with my wife;

And the muscular strength which it gave to my jaw
    Has lasted the rest of my life."

"You are old," said the youth; "one would hardly suppose
    That your eye was as steady as ever;
Yet you balanced an eel on the end of your nose—
    What made you so awfully clever?"

"I have answered three questions, and that is enough,"
    Said his father, "don't give yourself airs!
Do you think I can listen all day to such stuff?
    Be off, or I'll kick you downstairs!"

Lewis Carroll

WYNKEN, BLYNKEN, AND NOD

Wynken, Blynken, and Nod one night
    Sailed off in a wooden shoe—
Sailed on a river of crystal light,
    Into a sea of dew.
"Where are you going, and what do you wish?"
    The old moon asked the three.
"We have come to fish for the herring fish
    That live in this beautiful sea;
    Nets of silver and gold have we!"
              Said Wynken,
              Blynken,
              And Nod.

The old moon laughed and sang a song,
    As they rocked in the wooden shoe,
And the wind that sped them all night long
    Ruffled the waves of dew.

The little stars were the herring fish
    That lived in that beautiful sea—
"Now cast your nets wherever you wish—
    Never afeared are we";
So cried the stars to the fishermen three:
            Wynken,
            Blynken,
            And Nod.

All night long their nets they threw
        To the stars in the twinkling foam—
Then down from the skies came the wooden shoe,
    Bringing the fishermen home;
'Twas all so pretty a sail it seemed
    As if it could not be,
And some folks thought 'twas a dream they'd dreamed
    Of sailing that beautiful sea—
    But I shall name you the fishermen three:
            Wynken,
            Blynken,
            And Nod.

Wynken and Blynken are two little eyes,
    And Nod is a little head,
And the wooden shoe that sailed the skies
    Is a wee one's trundle-bed.
So shut your eyes while mother sings
    Of wonderful sights that be,
And you shall see the beautiful things
    As you rock in the misty sea,
    Where the old shoe rocked the fishermen three:
            Wynken,
            Blynken,
            And Nod.

                                    Eugene Field

MINIVER CHEEVY

Miniver Cheevy, child of scorn,
   Grew lean while he assailed the seasons;
He wept that he was ever born,
   And he had reasons.

Miniver loved the days of old
   When swords were bright and steeds were prancing;
The vision of a warrior bold
   Would set him dancing.

Miniver sighed for what was not,
   And dreamed, and rested from his labors;
He dreamed of Thebes and Camelot,
   And Priam's neighbors.

Miniver mourned the ripe renown
   That made so many a name so fragrant;
He mourned Romance, now on the town;
   And Art, a vagrant.

Miniver loved the Medici,
   Albeit he had never seen one;
He would have sinned incessantly
   Could he have been one.

Miniver cursed the commonplace
   And eyed a khaki suit with loathing;
He missed the medieval grace
   Of iron clothing.

Miniver scorned the gold he sought,
   But sore annoyed was he without it;

Miniver thought, and thought, and thought,
  And thought about it.

Miniver Cheevy, born too late,
    Scratched his head and kept on thinking;
Miniver coughed, and called it fate,
  And kept on drinking.
                              Edwin Arlington Robinson

A TRAGIC STORY

There lived a sage in days of yore,
And he a handsome pigtail wore;
But wondered much and sorrowed more,
  Because it hung behind him.

He mused upon this curious case,
And swore he'd change the pigtail's place,
And have it hanging at his face,
  Not dangling there behind him.

Says he, "The mystery I've found,—
I'll turn me round,"—he turned him round;
  But still it hung behind him.
Then round and round, and out and in,
All day the puzzled sage did spin;

In vain—it mattered not a pin,—
  The pigtail hung behind him.

And right and left, and round about,
And up and down, and in and out,

He turned; but still the pigtail stout
    Hung steadily behind him.

And though his efforts never slack,
And though he twist and twirl and tack,
Alas! still faithful to his back,
    The pigtail hangs behind him.
              William Makepeace Thackeray

THE GREAT PANJANDRUM

So she went into the garden
to cut a cabbage-leaf
to make an apple-pie;
and at the same time
a great she-bear, coming down the street,
pops its head into the shop.
What! no soap?
          So he died,
and she very imprudently married the Barber:
and there were present
the Picninnies,
      and the Joblillies,
         And the Garyulies,
and the great Panjandrum himself,
with the little round button at top;
and they all fell to playing the game of catch-as-catch-can,
till the gunpowder ran out at the heels of their boots.
              Samuel Foote

Mysteries

ABOU BEN ADHEM

Abou Ben Adhem (may his tribe increase!)
Awoke one night from a deep dream of peace,
And saw, within the moonlight in his room,
Making it rich, and like a lily in bloom,
An angel writing in a book of gold.
Exceeding peace had made Ben Adhem bold,
And to the presence in the room he said:
'What writest thou?'—The vision raised its head,
And with a look made of all sweet accord,
Answered: 'The names of those who love the Lord.'

'And is mine one?' said Abou. 'Nay, not so,'
Replied the angel. Abou spoke more low,
But cheerly still, and said: 'I pray thee, then,
Write me as one that loves his fellow-men.'
The angel wrote, and vanished. The next night
It came again with a great wakening light,
And showed the names whom love of God had bless'd,
And lo! Ben Adhem's name led all the rest!

Leigh Hunt

from AUGURIES OF INNOCENCE

To see a World in a Grain of Sand
And a Heaven in a Wild Flower
Hold Infinity in the palm of your hand
And Eternity in an hour.

William Blake

THE CAPTAIN'S DAUGHTER

We were crowded in the cabin,
  Not a soul would dare to sleep,—
It was midnight on the waters,
  And a storm was on the deep.

'Tis a fearful thing in winter
  To be shattered by the blast,
And to hear the rattling trumpet
  Thunder, "Cut away the mast!"

So we shuddered there in silence,—
  For the stoutest held his breath,
While the hungry sea was roaring,
  And the breakers talked with Death.

As thus we sat in darkness,
  Each one busy with his prayers,
"We are lost!" the captain shouted,
  As he staggered down the stairs.

But his little daughter whispered,
  As she took his icy hand,
"Isn't God upon the ocean,
  Just the same as on the land?"

Then we kissed the little maiden,
  And we spoke in better cheer,
And we anchored safe in harbor
  When the morn was shining clear.
                    James Thomas Fields

From 'TWO GENTLEMEN OF VERONA'

(ACT IV. SCENE 2)

Who is Silvia? What is she,
    That all our swains commend her?
Holy, fair, and wise is she;
    The heaven such grace did lend her,
That she might admirèd be.

Is she kind as she is fair,—
    For beauty lives with kindness?
Love doth to her eyes repair,
    To help him of his blindness;
And, being helped, inhabits there.

Then to Silvia let us sing
    That Silvia is excelling;
She excels each mortal thing
    Upon the dull earth dwelling;
To her let us garlands bring.

William Shakespeare

WITCHES' CHARM

The owl is abroad, the bat and the toad,
    And so is the cat-a-mountain;
The ant and the mole sit both in a hole,
    And frog peeps out o' the fountain.
The dogs they do bay, and the timbrels play,
    The spindles is now a-turning;
The moon it is red, and the stars are fled,

But all the sky is a-burning:
The ditch is made, and our nails the spade:
With pictures full, of wax and of wool,
Their livers I stick with needles quick;
There lacks but the blood to make up the flood.
Quickly, dame, then bring your part in!
Spur, spur, upon little Martin!
Merrily, merrily, make him sail,
A worm in his mouth and a thorn in's tail,
Fire above, and fire below,
With a whip i' your hand to make him go!

Ben Jonson

QUESTION

The man in the wilderness said to me,
How many strawberries grow in the sea?
I answered him as I thought good,
As many red herrings as grow in the wood.

Anonymous

A SLUMBER DID MY SPIRIT SEAL

A slumber did my spirit seal;
   I had no human fears:
She seemed a thing that could not feel
   The touch of earthly years.

No motion has she now, no force;
   She neither hears nor sees;
Rolled round in earth's diurnal course,
   With rocks, and stones, and trees.

William Wordsworth

from SONG'S ETERNITY

What is song's eternity?
  Come and see.
Can it noise and bustle be?
  Come and see.
Praises sung or praises said
  Can it be?
Wait awhile and these are dead—
  Sigh—sigh;
Be they high or lowly bred
  They die.

What is song's eternity?
  Come and see.
Melodies of earth and sky,
  Here they be.
Song once sung tc Adam's ears
  Can it be?
Ballads of six thousand years
  · Thrive, thrive;
Songs awaken with the spheres
  Alive.

* * * *

'*Tootle tootle tootle tee*'—
  Can it be
Pride and fame must shadows be?
  Come and see—
Every season own her own;
  Bird and bee
Sing creation's music in;
  Nature's glee
Is in every mood and tone
  Eternity.

                              John Clare

THE EAGLE

He clasps the crag with crooked hands;
Close to the sun in lonely lands,
Ring'd with the azure world, he stands.

The wrinkled sea beneath him crawls;
He watches from his mountain walls,
And like a thunderbolt he falls.

Lord Tennyson

A CHILD'S THOUGHT OF GOD

They say that God lives very high,
    But if you look above the pines
You cannot see our God, and why?

And if you dig down in the mines
    You never see Him in the gold;
Though, from Him, all that's glory shines.

God is so good, He wears a fold
    Of heaven and earth across His face—
Like secrets kept, for love, untold.

But still I feel that His embrace
    Slides down by thrills, through all things made,
Through sight and sound of every place.

As if my tender mother laid
    On my shut lids, her kisses' pressure,
Half-waking me at night, and said,
    "Who kissed you through the dark, dear guesser?"
                Elizabeth Barrett Browning

IN A MOONLIGHT WILDERNESS

Encintured with a twine of leaves,
That leafy twine his only dress!
A lovely Boy was plucking fruits,
By moonlight, in a wilderness.
The moon was bright, the air was free,
And fruits and flowers together grew
On many a shrub and many a tree:
And all put on a gentle hue,

Hanging in the shadowy air
Like a picture rich and rare.
It was a climate where, they say,
The night is more belov'd than day.
But who that beauteous Boy beguil'd,
That beauteous Boy, to linger here?
Alone, by night, a little child,
In place so silent and so wild—
Has he no friend, no loving mother near?

Samuel Taylor Coleridge

THIS IS THE KEY

This is the key of the kingdom:
In that kingdom there is a city.
In that city there is a town.
In that town there is a street.
In that street there is a lane.
In that lane there is a yard.
In that yard there is a house.
In that house there is a room.
In that room there is a bed.
On that bed there is a basket.
In that basket there are some flowers.
Flowers in a basket.
Basket in the bed.
Bed in the room.
Room in the house.
House in the yard.
Yard in the lane.
Lane in the street.
Street in the town.
Town in the city.
City in the kingdom.
Of the kingdom this is the key.

Anonymous

ELDORADO

Gaily bedight,
A gallant knight,
In sunshine and in shadow,
Had journeyed long,
Singing a song,
In search of Eldorado.

But he grew old—
This knight so bold—
And o'er his heart a shadow
Fell, as he found
No spot of ground
That looked like Eldorado.

And, as his strength
Failed him at length,
He met a pilgrim shadow—
'Shadow,' said he,
'Where can it be—
This land of Eldorado?'

'Over the Mountains
Of the Moon,
Down the Valley of the Shadow,
Ride, boldly ride,'
The shade replied,
'If you seek for Eldorado!'

Edgar Allan Poe

HEY HOW

Hey-How for Hallowe'en!
A the witches tae be seen,
Some black, an some green,
Hey-how for Hallowe'en!

Anonymous

THE MOON

And, like a dying lady lean and pale,
Who totters forth, wrapp'd in a gauzy veil,
Out of her chamber, led by the insane
And feeble wanderings of her fading brain,
The moon arose up in the murky east
A white and shapeless mass.

Art thou pale for weariness
Of climbing heaven and gazing on the earth,
Wandering companionless
Among the stars that have a different birth,
And ever changing, like a joyless eye
That finds no object worth its constancy?

P. B. Shelley

I SAW

I saw a peacock with a fiery tail
I saw a blazing comet drop down hail
I saw a cloud wrapped with ivy round
I saw an oak creep upon the ground
I saw a pismire swallow up a whale
I saw the sea brimful of ale
I saw a Venice glass full fifteen feet deep
I saw a well full of men's tears that weep
I saw red eyes all of a flaming fire
I saw a house bigger than the moon and higher
I saw the sun at twelve o'clock at night
I saw the man that saw this wondrous sight.

Anonymous

People
Who Used to Be

THE VILLAGE BLACKSMITH

Under a spreading chestnut tree
   The village smithy stands;
The smith, a mighty man is he,
   With large and sinewy hands;
And the muscles of his brawny arms
   Are strong as iron bands.

His hair is crisp, and black, and long,
   His face is like the tan;
His brow is wet with honest sweat,
   He earns whate'er he can,
And looks the whole world in the face,
   For he owes not any man.

Week in, week out, from morn till night,
   You can hear his bellows blow;
You can hear him swing his heavy sledge,
   With measured beat and slow,
Like a sexton ringing the village bell,
   When the evening sun is low.

And children coming home from school
   Look in at the open door;
They love to see the flaming forge,
   And hear the bellows roar,
And catch the burning sparks that fly
   Like chaff from a threshing-floor.

He goes on Sunday to the church,
   And sits among his boys;
He hears the parson pray and preach,
   He hears his daughter's voice,
Singing in the village choir,
   And it makes his heart rejoice.

It sounds to him like her mother's voice,
  Singing in Paradise!
He needs must think of her once more,
  How in the grave she lies;
And with his hard, rough hand he wipes
A tear out of his eyes.

Toiling,—rejoicing,—sorrowing,
  Onward through life he goes;
Each morning sees some task begun,
  Each evening sees its close;
Something attempted, something done,
  Has earned a night's repose.

Thanks, thanks to thee, my worthy friend,
  For the lesson thou hast taught!
Thus at the flaming forge of life
  Our fortunes must be wrought;
Thus on its sounding anvil shaped
  Each burning deed and thought!
                    Henry W. Longfellow

THE OLD TRAMP

Old Tramp slep' in our stable wunst,
  An' The Raggedy Man he caught
An' roust hi mup, and chased him off
  Clean out through our back lot!
An' th' Old Tramp hollered back an' said,—
  "You're a *purty* man—*You* air!—
With a pair o' eyes like two fried eggs,
  An' a nose like a Barlutt pear!"
                    James Whitcomb Riley

SIR GEOFFREY CHAUCER

His stature was not very tall,
Laen he was, his legs were small,
Hosed within a stock of red,
A buttoned bonnet on his head,
From under which did hang, I ween,
Silver hairs both bright and sheen.
His beard was white, trimmed round,
His countenance blithe and merry found.
A sleeveless jacket large and wide,
With many plights and skirts side,
Of water camlet did he wear;
A whittle by his belt he bare,
His shoes were corned, broad before,
His inkhorn at his side he wore,
And in his hand he bore a book.
Thus did this ancient poet look.

Robert Greene

side, long   *whittle*, knife   *corned*, peaked
camlet, material made of hair

WHEN ALYSANDYR OUR KING WAS DEDE

When Alysandyr our King was dede
   That Scotland led in luve and le,
Away was sons of ale and brede,
   Of wine and wax, of gamyn and gle;
Our gold was changyd into lede.
   Christ born into Virginitie
Succour Scotland and remede
   That stad is in perplexytie.

Anonymous

le, law   *sons*, plenty   *gamyn*, sport,   *stad*, stayed

ELEGY ON THE DEATH OF A MAD DOG

Good people all, of every sort,
   Give ear unto my song;
And if you find it wondrous short,
   It cannot hold you long.

In Islington there was a man,
  Of whom the world might say,
That still a godly race he ran,
  Whene'er he went to pray.

A kind and gentle heart he had,
  To comfort friends and foes;
The naked every day he clad,
  When he put on his clothes.

And in that town a dog was found,
  As many dogs there be,
Both mongrel, puppy, whelp, and hound,
  And curs of low degree.

This dog and man at first were friends;
  But when a pique began,
The dog, to gain some private ends,
  Went mad and bit the man.

Around from all the neighboring streets
  The wondering neighbors ran,
And swore the dog had lost his wits,
  To bite so good a man.

The wound it seem'd both sore and sad
  To every Christian eye;
And while they swore the dog was mad,
  They swore the man would die.

But soon a wonder came to light,
  That show'd the rogues they lied:
The man recover'd of the bite,
    The dog it was that died.

                              Oliver Goldsmith

SELF-PORTRAIT OF
THE LAUREATE OF NONSENSE

How pleasant to know Mr. Lear!
   Who has written such volumes of stuff!
Some think him ill-tempered and queer,
   But a few think him pleasant enough.

His mind is concrete and fastidious,
   His nose is remarkably big;
His visage is more or less hideous,
   His beard it resembles a wig.

He has ears, and two eyes, and ten fingers,
   Leastways, if you reckon two thumbs;
Long ago he was one of the singers,
   But now he is one of the dumbs.

He sits in a beautiful parlor,
   With hundreds of books on the wall;
He drinks a great deal of Marsala,
   But never gets tipsy at all.

He has many friends, laymen and clerical;
   Old Foss is the name of his cat;
His body is perfectly spherical,
   He weareth a runcible hat.

When he walks in a waterproof white,
   The children run after him so!
Calling out, 'He's come out in his night-
   Gown, that crazy old Englishman, oh!'

He weeps by the side of the ocean,
   He weeps on the top of the hill;

He purchases pancakes and lotion,
  And chocolate shrimps from the mill.

He reads but he cannot speak Spanish,
  He cannot abide ginger-beer:
Ere the days of his pilgrimage vanish,
  How pleasant to know Mr. Lear!
                              Edward Lear

LITTLE ORPHANT ANNIE

Little Orphant Annie's come to our house to stay,
An' wash the cups an' saucers up, an' brush the crumbs
        away,
An' shoo the chickens off the porch, an' dust the hearth,
        an' sweep,
An' make the fire, an' bake the bread, an' earn her board-
        an'-keep;
An' all us other childern, when the supper things is done,
We set around the kitchen fire an' has the mostest fun
A-list'nin' to the witch-tales 'at Annie tells about,
An' the Gobble-uns 'at gits you
          Ef you
            Don't
              Watch
                Out!

Onc't they was a little boy wouldn't say his prayers,—
So when he went to bed at night, away up stairs,
His Mammy heerd him holler, an' his Daddy heerd him
        bawl,
An' when they turn't the kivvers down, he wasn't there
        at all!
An' they seeked him in the rafter-room, an' cubby-hole,
        an' press,

An' seeked him up the chimbly-flue, an' ever'wheres, I guess;
But all they ever found was thist his pant's an' roundabout:—
An' the Gobble-uns'll git you

       Ef you
          Don't
             Watch
                Out!

An' one time a little girl 'ud allus laugh an' grin,
An' make fun of ever'one, an' all her blood an' kin;
An' onc't, when they was "company," an' ole folks was there,
She mocked 'em an' shocked 'em, an' said she didn't care!
An' thist as she kicked her heels, an' turn't to run an' hide,
They was two great big Black Things a-standin' by her side,
An' they snatched her through the ceilin' fore she knowed
      what's she's about!
An' the Gobble-uns'll git you
       Ef you
          Don't
             Watch
                Out!

An' little Orphant Annie says, when the blaze is blue,
An' the lamp-wick sputters, an' the wind goes *woo-oo!*
An' you hear the crickets quit, an' the moon is gray,
An' the lightnin'-bugs in dew is all squenched away,—
You better mind yer parents, an' yer teachers fond an' dear,
An' churish them 'at loves you, an' dry the orphant's tear,
An' he'p the pore an' needy ones 'at clusters all about,
Er the Gobble-uns'll git you
       Ef you
          Don't
             Watch
                Out!

James Whitcomb Riley

THERE WAS A BOY

There was a Boy; ye knew him well, ye cliffs
And islands of Winander!—many a time,
At evening, when the earliest stars began
To move along the edges of the hills,
Rising or setting, would he stand alone,
Beneath the trees, or by the glimmering lake;
And there, with fingers interwoven, both hands
Pressed closely palm to palm and to his mouth
Uplifted, he, as through an instrument,
Blew mimic hootings to the silent owls,
That they might answer him.—And they would shout
Across the watery vale, and shout again,
Responsive to his call,—with quivering peals,
And long halloos, and screams, and echoes loud
Redoubled and redoubled; concourse wild
Of jocund din! And, when there came a pause
Of silence such as baffled his best skill:
Then, sometimes, in that silence, while he hung
Listening, a gentle shock of mild surprise
Has carried far into his heart the voice
Of mountain-torrents; or the visible scene
Would enter unawares into his mind
With all its solemn imagery, its rocks,
Its woods, and that uncertain heaven received
Into the bosom of the steady lake.

William Wordsworth

WEE WILLIE WINKIE

Wee Willie Winkie rins through the toon,
Upstairs and downstairs in his nicht-goon,
Tirlin' at the window, crying at the lock,
'Are the weans in their bed, for it's now ten o'clock?'

'Hey, Willie Winkie, are ye comin' ben?
The cat's singing grey thrums to the sleepin' hen,
The dog's speldert on the floor, and disna gie a cheep,
But here's a waukrife laddie that wunna fa' asleep!

'Onything but sleep, you rogue! glow'ring like the moon,
Rattlin' in an airn jug wi' an airn spoon,
Rumblin', tumblin' roon about, crawin' like a cock,
Skirlin' like I kenna what, wauk'nin' sleeping' folk.

'Hey, Willie Winkie—the wean's in a creel!
Wamblin' aff a bodie's knee like a verra eel,
Ruggin' at the cat's lug, and ravelin' a' her thrums—
Hey, Willie Winkie—see, there he comes!'

Wearit is the mither that has a stoorie wean,
A wee stumpie stousie, that canna rin his lane,
That has a battle aye wi' sleep afore he'll close an e'e—
But a kiss frae aff his rosy lips gies strength anew to me.
                                                    William Miller

ON FIRST LOOKING INTO CHAPMAN'S HOMER

Much have I travell'd in the realms of gold,
    And many goodly states and kingdoms seen;
    Round many western islands have I been
Which bards in fealty to Apollo hold.
Oft of one wide expanse had I been told
    That deep-brow'd Homer ruled as his demesne;
    Yet did I never breathe its pure serene
Till I heard Chapman speak out loud and bold:
Then felt I like some watcher of the skies
    When a new planet swims into his ken;

Or like stout Cortez when with eagle eyes
    He star'd at the Pacific—and all his men
Look'd at each other with a wild surmise—
    Silent, upon a peak in Darien.

John Keats

THE RAGGEDY MAN

O The Raggedy Man! He works fer Pa;
An' he's the goodest man ever you saw!
He comes to our house every day,
An' waters the horses, an' feeds 'em hay;
An' he opens the shed—an' we all ist laugh
When he drives out our little old wobble-ly calf;
An' nen—ef our hired girls says he can—
He milks the cow fer 'Lizabuth Ann.—
    Ain't he a' awful good Raggedy Man?
        Raggedy! Raggedy! Raggedy Man!

W'y The Raggedy Man—he's ist so good
He splits the kindlin' an' chops the wood;
An' nen he spades in our garden, too,
An' does most things 'at *boys* can't do—
He climbed clean up in our big tree
An' shooked a' apple down fer me—
An' nother'n', too, fer 'Lizabuth Ann—
An' nother'n', too, fer The Raggedy Man.—
    Aint he a' awful kind Raggedy Man?
        Raggedy! Raggedy! Raggedy Man!

An' The Raggedy Man, he knows most rhymes
An' tells 'em, ef I be good, sometimes:
Knows 'bout Giunts, an' Griffuns, an' Elves,
An' the Squidgicum-Squees 'at swallers therselves!

An' wite by the pump in our pasture-lot,
He showed me the hole 'at the Wunks is got,
At lives 'way deep in the ground, an' can
Turn into me, er 'Lizabuth Ann!
   Aint he a funny old Raggedy Man?
     Raggedy! Raggedy! Raggedy Man!

The Raggedy Man—one time when he
Wuz makin' a little bow-'n'-orry fer me,
Says "When *you're* big like your Papa is,
Air you go' to keep a fine store like his—
An' be a rich merchant—an' wear fine clothes?—
Er what *air* you go' to be, goodness knows!"
An' nen he laughed at 'Lizabuth Ann,
An' I says "'M go' to be a Raggedy Man!—
   I'm ist go' to be a nice Raggedy Man!"
     Raggedy! Raggedy! Raggedy Man!
          James Whitcomb Riley

THE KNIGHT'S TOMB

Where is the grave of Sir Arthur O'Kellyn?
Where may the grave of that good man be?—
By the side of a spring, on the breast of Helvellyn,
Under the twigs of a young birch tree!
The oak that in summer was sweet to hear,
And rustled its leaves in the fall of the year,
And whistled and roared in the winter alone,
Is gone,—and the birch in its stead is grown.—
The Knight's bones are dust,
And his good sword rust;—
His soul is with the saints, I trust.
          Samuel Taylor Coleridge

THE LAMPLIGHTER

My tea is nearly ready and the sun has left the sky;
It's time to take the window to see Leerie going by;
For every night at teatime and before you take your seat,
With lantern and with ladder he comes posting up the street.

Now Tom would be a driver and Maria go to sea,
And my papa's a banker and as rich as he can be;
But I, when I am stronger and can choose what I'm to do,
I Leerie, I'll go round at night and light tht lamps with you!

For we are very lucky, with a lamp before the door,
And Leerie stops to light it as he lights so many more;
And O! before you hurry by with ladder and with light,
O Leerie, see a little child and nod to him tonight!

Robert Louis Stevenson

THE FORT OF RATHANGAN

The fort over against the oak-wood,
Once it was Bruidge's, it was Cathal's,
It was Aed's, it was Ailill's,
It was Conaing's, it was Cuiline's,
And it was Maeldúin's;
The fort remains after each in his turn—
And the kings asleep in the ground.

ANON: *translated from the
Irish by Kuno Meyer*

Small World

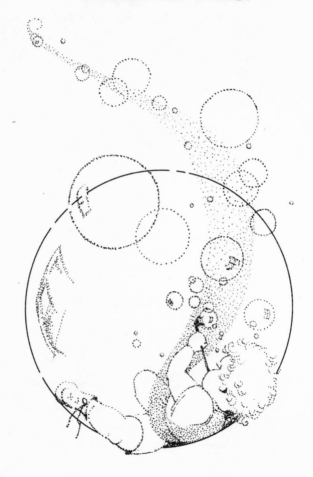

JEMIMA

There was a little girl, and she wore a little curl
    Right down the middle of her forehead
When she was good, she was very, very, good,
    But when she was bad, she was horrid!

One day she went upstairs, while her parents, unawares,
    In the kitchen down below were occupied with meals,
And she stood upon her head, on her little truckle bed,
    And she then began hurraying with her heels.

Her mother heard the noise, and thought it was the boys
    A-playing at a combat in the attic,
But when she climbed the stair and saw Jemima there,
    She took and she did her whip her most emphatic.

Anonymous

YOUNG NIGHT THOUGHT

All night long and every night,
When my mamma puts out the light,
I see the people marching by,
As plain as day, before my eye.

Armies and emperors and kings,
All carrying different kinds of things,
And marching in so grand a way,
You never saw the like by day.

So fine a show was never seen,
At the great circus on the green;
For every kind of beast and man
Is marching in that caravan.

At first they move a little slow,
But still the faster on they go,
And still beside them close I keep
Until we reach the town of Sleep.
                    Robert Louis Stevenson

FOREIGN CHILDREN

Little Indian, Sioux or Crow,
  Little frosty Eskimo,
  Little Turk or Japanee,
O! don't you wish that you were me?

You have seen the scarlet trees
And the lions over seas;
You have eaten ostrich eggs,
And turned the turtles off their legs.

Such a life is very fine,
But it's not so nice as mine:
You must often, as you trod,
Have wearied *not* to be abroad.

You have curious things to eat,
I am fed on proper meat;
You must dwell beyond the foam,
But I am safe and live at home.

Little Indian, Sioux or Crow,
  Little frosty Eskimo,
  Little Turk or Japanee,
O! don't you wish that you were me?
                    Robert Louis Stevenson

THE LAND OF COUNTERPANE

When I was sick and lay abed,
I had two pillows at my head,
And all my toys beside me lay
To keep me happy all the day.

And sometimes for an hour or so
I watched my leaden soldiers go,
With different uniforms and drills,
Among the bedclothes, through the hills;

And sometimes sent my ships in fleets
All up and down among the streets;
Or brought my trees and houses out,
And planted cities all about.

I was the giant great and still
That sits upon the pillow hill,
And sees before him, dale and plain,
The pleasant land of counterpane.

Robert Louis Stevenson

MY SHADOW

I have a little shadow that goes in and out with me,
And what can be the use of him is more than I can see.
He is very, very like me from the heels up to the head;
And I see him jump before me, when I jump into my bed.

The funniest thing about him is the way he likes to grow—
Not at all like proper children, which is always very slow;
For he sometimes shoots up taller like an india-rubber ball,
And he sometimes get so little that there's none of him at all.

He hasn't got a notion of how children ought to play,
And can only make a fool of me in every sort of way.
He stays so close beside me, he's a coward you can see;
I'd think shame to stick to nurse as that shadow sticks to me!

One morning, very early, before the sun was up,
I rose and found the shining dew on every buttercup;
But my lazy little shadow, like an arrant sleepyhead,
Had stayed at home behind me and was fast asleep in bed.

Robert Louis Stevenson

MARCHING SONG

Bring the comb and play upon it!
   Marching, here we come!
Willie cocks his highland bonnet,
   Johnnie beats the drum.

Mary Jane commands the party,
   Peter leads the rear;
Feet in time, alert and hearty,
   Each a Grenadier!

All in the most martial manner
   Marching double-quick;
While the napkin like a banner
   Waves upon the stick!

Here's enough of fame and pillage,
   Great commander Jane!
Now that we've been round the village
   Let's go home again.

Robert Louis Stevenson

SPEAK ROUGHLY TO YOUR LITTLE BOY

Speak roughly to your little boy,
    And beat him when he sneezes;
He only does it to annoy,
    Because he knows it teases.
        Wow! Wow! Wow!

I speak severely to my boy,
    I beat him when he sneezes;
For he can thoroughly enjoy
    The pepper when he pleases!
        Wow! Wow! Wow!
        Lewis Carroll

MONDAY'S CHILD

Monday's child is fair of face,
Tuesday's child is full of grace,
Wednesday's child is full of woe,
Thursday's child has far to go,
Friday's child is loving and giving,
Saturday's child works hard for his living,
And the child that is born on the Sabbath day
Is bonny and blithe, and good and gay.
        Anonymous

MY BED IS A BOAT

My bed is like a little boat;
    Nurse helps me in when I embark;
She girds me in my sailor's coat
    And starts me in the dark.

At night, I go on board and say
    Good night to all my friends on shore;
I shut my eyes and sail away
    And see and hear no more.

And sometimes things to bed I take,
    As prudent sailors have to do:
Perhaps a slice of wedding cake,
    Perhaps a toy or two.

All night across the dark we steer:
    But when the day returns at last
Safe in my room, beside the pier,
    I find my vessel fast.

Robert Louis Stevenson

THE SUN'S TRAVELS

The sun is not abed, when I
At night upon my pillow lie;
Still round the earth his way he takes,
And morning after morning makes.

While here at home, in shining day,
We round the sunny garden play,
Each little Indian sleepyhead
Is being kissed and put to bed.

And when at eve I rise from tea,
Day dawns beyond the Atlantic Sea,
And all the children in the West
Are getting up and being dressed.

Robert Louis Stevenson

THE COW

The friendly cow all red and white,
 I love with all my heart:
She gives me cream with all her might,
 To eat with apple tart.

She wanders lowing here and there,
 And yet she cannot stray,
All in the pleasant open air,
 The pleasant light of day;

And blown by all the winds that pass
 And wet with all the showers,
She walks among the meadow grass
 And eats the meadow flowers.
        Robert Louis Stevenson

HAPPY THOUGHT

The world is so full of a number of things,
I'm sure we should all be as happy as kings.

Robert Louis Stevenson

RAIN

The rain is raining all around,
It falls on field and tree,
It rains on the umbrella here,
And on the ships at sea.

Robert Louis Stevenson

TIME TO RISE

A BIRDIE with a yellow bill
Hopped upon the window sill,
Cocked his shining eye and said:
"Ain't you 'shamed, you sleepyhead?"

Robert Louis Stevenson

NAUGHTY CLAUDE

When Little Claude was naughty wunst
    At dinner-time, an' said
He wo'nt say *"Thank you"* to his Ma,
    She maked him go to bed
An' stay two hours an' not git up,—
    So when the clock struck Two,
Nen Claude says,—"Thank you, Mr. Clock,
    I'm much obleeged to you!"

James Whitcomb Riley

BED IN SUMMER

In winter I get up at night
And dress by yellow candlelight.
In summer, quite the other way,
I have to go to bed by day.

I have to go to bed and see
The birds still hopping on the tree,
Or hear the grown-up people's feet
Still going past me in the street.

And does it not seem hard to you,
When all the sky is clear and blue,
And I should like so much to play,
To have to go to bed by day?

Robert Louis Stevenson

A TERRIBLE INFANT

I recollect a nurse call'd Ann,
  Who carried me about the grass,
And one fine day a fine young man
  Came up, and kiss'd the pretty lass.

She did not make the least objection!
  Thinks I, *"Aha!*
When I can talk I'll tell Mamma"
—And that's my earliest recollection.

Frederick Locker-Lampson

Just for Laughs

POOR OLD LADY

Poor old lady, she swallowed a fly.
I don't know why she swallowed a fly.
Poor old lady, I think she'll die.

Poor old lady, she swallowed a spider.
It squirmed and wriggled an turned inside her.
She swallowed the spider to catch the fly.
I don't know why, *etc.*

Poor old lady, she swallowed a bird.
How absurd! She swallowed a bird.
She swallowed the bird to catch the spider,
She swallowed the spider to catch the fly, *etc.*

Poor old lady, she swallowed a cat.
Think of that! She swallowed a cat.
She swallowed the cat to catch the bird.
She swallowed the bird to catch the spider, *etc.*

Poor old lady, she swallowed a dog.
She went the whole hog when she swallowed the dog.
She swallowed the dog to catch the cat.
She swallowed the cat to catch the bird, *etc.*

Poor old lady, she swallowed a cow.
I don't know how she swallowed the cow.
She swallowed the cow to catch the dog, *etc.*

Poor old lady, she swallowed a horse.
She died, of course.

Anonymous

NIRVANA

I am
  A Clam!
Come learn of me
Unclouded peace and calm content,
  Serene, supreme tranquillity,
Where thoughtless dreams and dreamless thoughts are blent.

When the salt tide is rising to the flood,
  In billows blue my placid pulp I lave;
And when it ebbs I slumber in the mud,
  Content alike with ooze or crystal wave.

I do not shudder when in chowder stewed,
  Nor when the Coney Islander engulfs me raw.
When in the church soup's dreary solitude
  Alone I wander, do I shudder? Naw!

If jarring tempests beat upon my bed,
  Or summer peace there be,
I do not care: as I have said,
  All's one to me;
    A Clam
    I am.
          Anonymous

PEAS

I always eat peas with honey,
I've done it all my life,
They do taste kind of funny,
But it keeps them on the knife.
          Anonymous

HE THOUGHT HE SAW

He thought he saw an Elephant
  That practised on a fife:
He looked again, and found it was
  A letter from his wife.
"At length I realise," he said,
  "The bitterness of Life!"

He thought he saw a Buffalo
  Upon the chimney piece:
He looked again, and found it was
  His Sister's Husband's Niece.
"Unless you leave this house," he said,
  "I'll send for the Police!"

He thought he saw a Rattlesnake
  That questioned him in Greek:
He looked again, and found it was
  The Middle of Next Week.
  "The one thing I regret," he said,
  "Is that it cannot speak!"

He thought he saw a Banker's Clerk
  Descending from the bus:
He look again, and found it was
  A Hippopotamus:
"If this should stay to dine," he said,
  "There won't be much for us!"

He thought he saw an Albatross
  That fluttered round the lamp:
He looked again, and found it was
  A Penny-Postage-Stamp.

"You'd best be getting home," he said;
  "The nights are very damp!"

He thought he saw a Coach-and-Four
  That stood beside his bed:
He looked again, and found it was
  A Bear without a Head.
"Poor thing," he said, "poor silly thing!
  It's waiting to be fed!"

He thought he saw a Kangaroo
  That worked a coffee-mill:
He looked again, and found it was
  A Vegetable-Pill.
"Were I to swallow this," he said,
  "I should be very ill!"

Lewis Carroll

RHYME FOR A SIMPLETON

I said, "This horse, sir, will you shoe?"
  And soon the horse was shod.
I said, "This deed, sir, will you do?"
  And soon the deed was dod!

I said, "This stick, sir, will you break?"
  At once the stick he broke.
I said, "This coat, sir, will you make?"
  And soon the coat he moke!

Anonymous

WILLIE THE POISONER

Willie poisoned Auntie's tea,
Auntie died in agony.
Uncle came and looked quite vexed,
"Really, Will," said he, "what next?"
Anonymous

CARELESS WILLIE

Will, with a thirst for gore,
Nailed his sister to the door.
Mother said, with humor quaint:
"Now, Willie dear, don't scratch the paint."
Anonymous

SISTER NELL

In the family drinking well
Willie pushed his sister Nell.
She's there yet, because it kilt her—
Now we have to buy a filter.
Anonymous

WELL I NEVER

Well I never, did you ever,
See a monkey dressed in leather?
Leather eyes, leather nose,
Leather breeches to his toes.
Anonymous

THE WISHES OF AN ELDERLY MAN
Wished At A Garden Party, June 1914

I wish I loved the Human Race;
I wish I loved its silly face;
I wish I liked the way it walks;
I wish I liked the way it talks;
And when I'm introduced to one
I wish I thought *What Jolly Fun!*
                    Sir Walter Raleigh

O I C

I'm in a 10der mood today
    & feel poetic, 2;
4 fun I'll just—off a line
    & send it off 2 U.

I'm sorry you've been 6 o long;
    Don't B disconsol8;
But bear your ills with 42de,
    & they won't seen so gr8.
                    Anonymous

YOUNG SAMMY WATKINS

Young Sammy Watkins jumped out of bed;
    He ran to his sister and cut off her head.
This gave his dear mother a great deal of pain;
    She hopes that he never will do it again.
                    Anonymous

RUMBO AND JUMBO

Lord Rumbo was immensely rich
And he would stick at nothing.
He went about in golden boots
And silver underclothing

Lord Jumbo, on the other hand,
Though mentally acuter,
Could only run to silver boots,
His underclothes were pewter.

Anonymous

THERE WAS A YOUNG MAN OF ST. BEES

There was a young man of St. Bees
Who was stung on the arm by a wasp.
When they asked, "Does it hurt?"
He replied, "No, it doesn't,
But I thought all the time 'twas a hornet."

W. S. Gilbert

THERE WAS AN OLD STUPID
WHO WROTE

There was an old stupid who wrote
The verses above that we quote;
His want of all sense
Was something immense,
Which made him a person of note.

Walter Parke

THE HEIGHT OF THE RIDICULOUS

I wrote some lines once on a time
   In wondrous merry mood,
And thought, as usual, men would say
   They were exceeding good.

They were so queer, so very queer,
   I laughed as I would die;
Albeit, in the general way,
   A sober man am I.

I called my servant, and he came;
   How kind it was of him
To mind a slender man like me,
   He of the mighty limb.

"These to the printer," I exclaimed,
   And, in my humorous way,
I added (as a trifling jest),
   "There'll be the devil to pay."

He took the paper, and I watched,
   And saw him peep within;
At the first line he read, his face
   Was all upon the grin.

He read the next; the grin grew broad,
   And shot from ear to ear;
He read the third; a chuckling noise
   I now began to hear.

The fourth; he broke into a roar;
   The fifth; his waistband split;
The sixth; he burst five buttons off,
   And tumbled in a fit.

Ten days and nights, with sleepless eye,
  I watched that wretched man,
And since, I never dare to write
  As funny as I can.

Oliver Wendell Holmes

MR. FINNEY'S TURNIP

Mr. Finney had a turnip
  And it grew behind the barn;
And it grew and grew,
And that turnip did no harm.

There it grew and it grew
  Till it could grow no longer;
Then his daughter Lizzie picked it
  And put it in the cellar.

There it lay and it lay
  Till it began to rot;
And his daughter Suzie took it
  And put it in the pot.

And they boiled it and boiled it
  As long as they were able;
And then his daughters took it
  And put it on the able.

Mr. Finney and his wife
  They sat them down to sup;
And they ate and they ate
  And they ate that turnip up.

Anonymous

CONVERSATIONAL

"How's your father?" came the whisper,
  Bashful Ned the silence breaking;
"Oh, he's nicely," Annie murmured,
  Smilingly the question taking.

Conversation flagged a moment,
  Hopeless Ned essayed another:
"Annie, I—I," then a coughing,
  And the question, "Hows your mother?"

"Mother? Oh, she's doing finely!"
  Fleeting fast was all forbearance,
When in low, despairing accents,
  Came the climax, "How's your parents?"
                              Anonymous

TO BE OR NOT TO BE

I sometimes think I'd rather crow
And be a rooster than to roost
And be a crow. But I dunno.
A rooster he can roost also,
Which don't seem fair when crows can't crow.
Which may help some. Still I dunno.
Crows should be glad of one thing, though;
Nobody thinks of eating crow,
While roosters they are good enough
For anyone unless they're tough.
There are lots of tough old roosters, though,
And anyway a crow can't crow,
So mebby roosters stand more show.
It looks that way. But I dunno.
                              Anonymous

THERE WAS A YOUNG LADY WHOSE EYES

There was a Young Lady whose eyes
Were unique as to color and size;
   When she opened them wide,
   People all turned aside,
And started away in surprise.
                Edward Lear

NOSE, NOSE

Nose, nose, jolly red nose,
And who gave thee this jolly red nose?
Nutmegs and ginger, cinnamon and cloves
And they gave me this jolly red nose.
                Beaumont and Fletcher

JAYBIRD

Jaybird a-sitting on a hickory limb;
He winked at me and I winked at him.
I picked up a rock and hit him on the chin.
Say he, "Young feller, don't you do that again!"
                Anonymous

AS I WAS LAYING ON THE GREEN

As I was laying on the green,
A small English book I seen.
Carlyle's *Essay on Burns* was the edition,
So I left it laying in the same position.
                Anonymous

WHEN FATHER CARVES THE DUCK

We all look on with anxious eyes
    When father carves the duck,
And mother almost always sighs
    When father carves the duck;
Then all of us prepare to rise;
And hold our bibs before our eyes,
And be prepared for some surprise,
    When father carves the duck.

He braces up and grabs a fork
    Whene'er he carves a duck,
And won't allow a soul to talk
    Until he's carved the duck,
The fork is jabbed into the sides,
Across the breast the knife he slides,
While every careful person hides
    From flying chips of duck.

The platter's always sure to slip
    When father carves a duck,
And how it makes the dishes skip!
    Potatoes fly amuck!
The squash and cabbage leap in space,
We get some gravy in our face,
And father mutters Hindoo grace
    Whene'er he carves a duck.

We then have learned to walk around
    The dining room and pluck
From off the window sills and walls
    Our share of father's duck.
While father growls and blows and jaws

And swears the knife was full of flaws,
And mother laughs at him because
   He couldn't carve a duck.
E. V. Wright

THE PASSENJARE

The conductor when he receives a fare,
Must punch in the presence of the passenjare;
   A blue trip slip for a 8-cent fare,
   A buff trip slip for a 6-cent fare,
   A pink trip slip for a 3-cent fare,
All in the presence of the passenjare.
Punch, boys, punch, punch with care,
All in the presence of the passenjare.
Isaac H. Bromley

THE LITTLE PEACH

A little peach in the orchard grew
A little peach of emerald hue;
Warmed by the sun and wet by the dew,
   It grew.

One day, passing that orchard through,
That little peach dawned on the view
Of Johnny Jones and his sister Sue,
   Them two.
Up at that peach a club they threw,
Down from the stem on which it grew
Fell that peach of emerald hue.
   Mon Dieu!

John took a bite and Sue took a chew,
And then the trouble began to brew,
Trouble the doctor couldn't subdue.
    Too true!

Under the turf where the daisies grew
They planted John and his sister Sue,
And their little souls to the angels flew,
    Boo hoo!

What of that peach of the emerald hue;
Warmed by the sun and wet by the dew?
Ah, well, its mission on earth is through.
    Adieu!

Eugene Field

AUNT MAUD

I had written to Aunt Maud
Who was on a trip abroad,
When I heard she'd died of cramp
Just too late to save the stamp.

Anonymous

THE GIRL OF NEW YORK

There once was a girl of New York
Whose body was lighter than cork;
    She had to be fed
    For six weeks upon lead
Before she went out for a walk.

Cosmo Monkhouse

HOW DOTH THE LITTLE CROCODILE

How doth the little crocodile
  Improve his shining tail;
And pour the waters of the Nile
  On every golden scale!

How cheerfully he seems to grin,
  How neatly spreads his claws,
And welcomes little fishes in,
  With gently smiling jaws!
Lewis Carroll

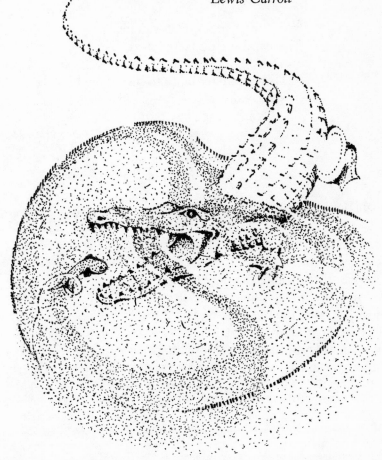

AS I WAS STANDING IN THE STREET

As I was standing in the street,
　　As quiet as could be,
A great big ugly man came up
　　And tied his horse to me.

A CENTIPEDE WAS HAPPY QUITE

A centipede was happy quite,
　　Until a frog in fun
Said, "Pray, which leg comes after which?"
This raised her mind to such a pitch,
She lay distracted in the ditch
　　Considering how to run.

THE COMMON CORMORANT

The common cormorant or shag
Lays eggs inside a paper bag.
The reason you will see no doubt
It is to keep the lightning out.
But what these unobservant birds
Have never noticed is that herds
Of wandering bears may come with buns
And steal the bags to hold the crumbs.

I'M A LITTLE HINDOO

I'm a little Hindoo,
I do all I kindoo.
Where my pants and shirt don't meet
I make my little skindoo.

Anonymous

THE PURPLE COW

I never saw a Purple Cow,
I never hope to see one,
But I can tell you, anyhow,
I'd rather see than be one!

Anonymous

THE PESSIMIST

Nothing to do but work,
    Nothing to eat but food,
Nothing to wear but clothes
    To keep one from going nude.

Nothing to breathe but air,
    Quick as a flash 't is gone;
Nowhere to fall but off,
    Nowhere to stand but on.

Nothing to comb but hair,
    Nowhere to sleep but in bed,
Nothing to weep but tears,
    Nothing to bury but dead.

Nothing to sing but songs,
   Ah, well, alast alack!
Nowhere to go but out,
   Nowhere to come but back.

Nothing to see but sights,
   Nothing to quench but thirst,
Nothing to have but what we've got;
   Thus thro' life we are cursed.

Nothing to strike but a gait;
   Everything moves that goes.
Nothing at all but common sense
   Can ever withstand these woes.

Ben King

GET UP, GET UP

Get up, get up, you lazy-head,
   Get up you lazy sinner,
We need those sheets for tablecloths,
   It's nearly time for dinner!

Anonymous

THERE WAS AN OLD PERSON OF DUNDALK

There was an old person of Dundalk,
Who tried to teach fishes to walk;
   When they tumbled down dead,
   He grew weary and said,
"I had better go back to Dundalk!"

Edward Lear

IF I SHOULD DIE TONIGHT

If I should die tonight
And you should come to my cold corpse and say,
Weeping and heartsick o'er my lifeless clay—
    If I should die tonight,
And you should come in deepest grief and woe—
And say: "Here's that ten dollars that I owe,"
    I might arise in my large white cravat
    And say, "What's that?"
    If I should die tonight
And you should come to my cold corpse and kneel,
Clasping my bier to show the grief you feel,
    I say, if I should die tonight
And you should come to me, and there and then
Just even hint 'bout paying me that ten,
    I might arise the while,
    But I'd drop dead again.

                                        Ben King

STATELY VERSE

If Mary goes far out to sea,
    By wayward breezes fanned,
I'd like to know—can you tell me?—
    Just where would Maryland?

If Tenny went high up in air
    And looked o'er land and lea,
Looked here and there and everywhere
    Pray what would Tennessee?

I looked out of the window and
    Saw Orry on the lawn;
He's not there now, and who can tell
    Just where has Oregon?

Two girls were quarrelling one day
    With garden tools, and so
I said, "My dears, let Mary rake
    And just let Idaho."

A friend of mine lived in a flat
    With half a dozen boys;
When he fell ill I asked him why.
    He said: "I'm Illinois."

An English lady had a steed.
    She called him 'Ighland Bay.
She rode for exercise, and thus
    Rhode Island every day.

                              Anonymous

A MORTIFYING MISTAKE

I studied my tables over and over, and backward and forward,
    too;
But I couldn't remember six times nine, and I didn't know
    what to do,
Till sister told me to play with my doll, and not to bother my
    head,
"If you call her 'Fifty-four' for a while, you'll learn it by heart,"
    she said.
So I took my favorite, Mary Ann (though I thought 'twas a
    dreadful shame
To give such a perfectly lovely child such a perfectly horrid
    name),
And I called her my dear little "Fifty-four" a hundred times,
    till I knew
The answer of six times nine as well as the answer of two
    times two.

Next day Elizabeth Wigglesworth, who always acts so proud,
Said, "Six times nine is Fifty-two," and I nearly laughed
aloud!
But I wished I hadn't when teacher said, "Now Dorothy, tell
if you can."
For I thought of my doll and—sakes alive!—I answered, "*Mary
Ann!*"

Anna M. Pratt

LIMERICKS

An epicure, dining at Crewe,
Found quite a large mouse in his stew.
　Said the waiter, "Don't shout,
　And wave it about,
Or the rest will be wanting one, too!"

There was an old man from Antigua,
Whose wife said, "My dear, what a pig you are!"
　He replied, "O my queen,
　Is it manners you mean,
Or do you refer to my fig-u-a?"

A maiden caught stealing a dahlia,
Said, "Oh, you shan't tell on me, shahlia?"
　But the florist was hot,
　And he said, "Like as not
They'll send you to jail, you bad gahlia."

A flea and a fly in a flue
Were imprisoned, so what could they do?
  Said the fly, "Let us flee,"
Said the flea, "Let us fly,"
So they flew through a flaw in the flue.

              There was an old person of Tring
              Who, when somebody asked her to sing,
                  Replied, "Isn't it odd?
                  I can never tell *God*
              Save the Weasel from *Pop Goes the King!*"

There was an old man of Blackheath,
Who sat on his set of false teeth.
  Said he, with a start,
  "O Lord, bless my heart!
I've bitten myself underneath!"

              A silly young fellow named Hyde
              In a funeral procession was spied;
                  When asked, "Who is dead?"
                  He giggled and said,
              "I don't know; I just came for the ride."

A boy who played tunes on a comb,
Had become such a nuisance at homb,
  That ma spanked him, and then—
  "Will you do it again?"
And he cheerfully answered her, "Nomb."

A decrepit old gasman, named Peter,
While hunting around for the meter,
    Touched a leak with his light;
    He rose out of sight—
And, as everyone who knows anything about poetry can tell
    you, he also ruined the meter.

Anonymous

THE PRODIGAL EGG

An egg of humble sphere
    By vain ambition stung,
Once left his mother dear
    When he was very young.

'Tis needless to dilate
    Upon a tale so sad;
The egg, I grieve to state,
    Grew very, very bad.

At last when old and blue,
    He wandered home, and then
They gently broke it to
    The loving mother hen.

She only said, in fun,
"I fear you're spoiled, my son!"

Anonymous

THERE WAS AN OLD MAN WITH A BEARD

There was an Old Man with a beard,
Who said, "It is just as I feared!—
   Two Owls and a Hen,
   Four Larks and a Wren,
Have all built their nests in my beard!"
                              Edward Lear

THE MICROBES

Two microbes sat on a pantry shelf
   And watched, with expressions pained,
      The milkmaid's stunts;
      And both said at once,
"Our relations are going to be strained."
                              Anonymous

THERE WAS AN OLD MAN OF IBREEM

There was an old man of Ibreem,
Who suddenly threatened to scream:
   But they said, "If you do,
   We will thump you quite blue,
You disgusting old man of Ibreem."
                              Edward Lear

THE KILKENNY CATS

There wanst was two cats at Kilkenny,
Each thought there was one cat too many,
   So they quarrell'd and fit,
   They scratch'd and they bit,
   Till, excepting their nails,
   And the tips of their tails,
Instead of two cats, there warnt any.
Anonymous

THE BARBER OF KEW

There once was a barber of Kew,
Who went very mad at the Zoo;
   He tried to enamel
   The face of the camel,
And gave the brown bear a shampoo.
Cosmo Monkhouse

THERE WAS A YOUNG
PRINCE IN BOMBAY

There was a young prince in Bombay,
Who always would have his own way;
   He pampered his horses
   On five or six courses,
Himself eating nothing but hay.
Anonymous

Wise Words

A DAY IN JUNE
(From *The Vision of Sir Launfal*)

For a cap and bells our lives we pay,
Bubbles we buy with a whole soul's tasking:
'Tis heaven alone that is given away,
'Tis only God may be had for the asking;
No price is set on the lavish summer;
June may be had by the poorest comer.
And what is so rare as a day in June?
  Then, if ever, come perfect days;
Then Heaven tries earth if it be in tune,
  And over it softly her warm ear lays;
Whether we look, or whether we listen,
We hear life murmur, or see it glisten;
Every clod feels a stir of might,
  An instinct within it that reaches and towers,
And, groping blindly above it for light,
  Climbs to a soul in grass and flowers;
The flush of life may well be seen
  Thrilling back over hills and valleys;
The cowslip startles in meadows green,
  The buttercup catches the sun in its chalice,
And there's never a leaf nor a blade too mean
  To be some happy creature's palace;
The little bird sits at his door in the sun,
  Atilt like a blossom among the leaves,
And lets his illumined being o'errun
  With the deluge of summer it receives;
His mate feels the eggs beneath her wings,
And the heart in her dumb breast flutters and sings;
He sings to the wide world, and she to her nest,—
In the nice ear of Nature which song is the best?

James Russell Lowell

WHERE THERE'S A WILL THERE'S A WAY

It was a noble Roman,
   In Rome's imperial day,
Who heard a coward croaker.
   Before the Castle, say:
"They're safe in such a fortress;
   There is no way to shake it!"
"On—on!" exclaimed the hero,
   "I'll find a way, or make it!"

Is *Fame* your aspiration?
   Her path is steep and high;
In vain he seeks her temple,
   Content to gaze and sigh:
The shining throne is waiting,
   But he alone can take it
Who says, with Roman firmness,
   "I'll find a way, or make it!"

Is *Learning* your ambition?
   There is no royal road;
Alike the peer and peasant
   Must climb to her abode:
Who feels the thirst of knowledge,
   In Helicon may slake it,
If he has still the Roman will
   "I'll find a way, or make it!"

Are *Riches* worth the getting?
   They must be bravely sought;
With wishing and with fretting
   The boon cannot be bought:
To all the prize is open,
   But only he can take it

Who says, with Roman courage,
"*I'll find a way, or make it!*"

In *Love's* impassioned warfare
    The tale has ever been,
That victory crowns the valiant,—
    The brave are they who win:
Though strong is Beauty's castle,
    A lover still may take it,
Who says, with Roman courage,
    "*I'll find a way, or make it!*"
                    John Godfrey Saxe

KINDNESS TO ANIMALS

Little children, never give
Pain to things that feel and live:
Let the gentle robin come
For the crumbs you save at home,—
As his meat you throw along
He'll repay you with a song;
Never hurt the timid hare
Peeping from her green grass lair,
Let her come and sport and play
On the lawn at close of day;
The little lark goes soaring high
To the bright windows of the sky,
Singing as if 'twere always spring,
And fluttering on an untired wing,—
Oh! let him sing his happy song,
Nor do these gentle creatures wrong.
                    Anonymous

SHEPHERD BOY'S SONG

He that is down, needs fear no fall;
   He that is low, no pride:
He that is humble, ever shall
   Have God to be his guide.

I am content with what I have,
   Little be it or much;
And, Lord, contentment still I crave,
   Because Thou savest such.

Fulness to such a burden is,
   That go on pilgrimage;
Here little, and hereafter bliss,
   Is best from age to age.

John Bunyan

A THOUGHT

It is very nice to think
The world is full of meat and drink,
With little children saying grace
In every Christian kind of place.

Robert Louis Stevenson

WHOLE DUTY OF CHILDREN

A child should always say what's true
And speak when he is spoken to,
And behave mannerly at table;
At least as far as he is able.

Robert Louis Stevenson

A ROUND

Hey nonny no!
Men are fools that wish to die!
Is't not fine to dance and sing
When the bells of death do ring?
Is't not fine to swim in wine,
And turn upon the toe,
And sing hey nonny no!
When the winds blow and the seas flow?
Hey nonny no!

Anonymous

GOOD AND BAD CHILDREN

Children, you are very little,
And your bones are very brittle;
If you would grow great and stately,
You must try to walk sedately.

You must still be bright and quiet,
And content with simple diet;
And remain, through all bewild'ring,
Innocent and honest children.

Happy hearts and happy faces,
Happy play in grassy places—
That was how, in ancient ages,
Children grew to kings and sages.

But the unkind and the unruly,
And the sort who eat unduly,
They must never hope for glory—
Theirs is quite a different story!

Cruel children, crying babies,
All grow up as geese and gabies,
Hated, as their age increases,
By their nephews and their nieces.
Robert Louis Stevenson

WHEN THAT I WAS

When that I was and a little tiny boy,
    With hey, ho, the wind and the rain;
A foolish thing was but a toy,
    For the rain it raineth every day.

But when I came to man's estate,
    With hey, ho, the wind and the rain;
'Gainst knaves and thieves men shut their gate,
    For the rain it raineth every day.

But when I came, alas! to wive,
    With hey, ho, the wind and the rain;
By swaggering could I never thrive,
    For the rain it raineth every day.

But when I came unto my beds,
    With hey, ho, the wind and the rain;
With toss-pots still had drunken heads,
    For the rain it raineth every day.

A great while ago the world begun,
    With hey, ho, the wind and the rain;
But that's all one, our play is done,
    And we'll strive to please you every day.
William Shakespeare

TO DAFFODILS

Fair daffodils, we weep to see
  You haste away so soon;
As yet the early-rising sun
  Has not attain'd his noon.
    Stay, stay
  Until the hasting day
    Has run
  But to the evensong;
And, having pray'd together, we
  Will go with you along.

We have short time to stay, as you,
  We have as short a spring;
As quick a growth to meet decay,
  As you, or anything.
    We die
  As your hours do, and dry
    Away
  Like to the summer's rain;
Or as the pearls of morning's dew,
  Ne'er to be found again.
          Robert Herrick

THREE THINGS

Three things are given man to do—
To dare, to labor and to grow:
Not otherwise from earth we came,
No otherwise our way we go.
Bliss Carman

TO HIS SON, VINCENT CORBET

*on his Birth-Day, November 10, 1630,
being then three years old*

What I shall leave thee none can tell,
But all shall say I wish thee well;
I wish thee, Vin, before all wealth,
Both bodily and ghostly health:
Nor too much wealth, nor wit, come to thee;
So much of either may undo thee.
I wish thee learning, not for show,
Enough for to instruct, and know;
Not such as gentlemen require,
To prate at table or at fire.
I wish thee all thy mother's graces,
Thy father's fortunes and his places.
I wish thee friends, and one at court,
Not to build on, but support;
To keep thee, not in doing many
Oppressions, but from suffering any.
I wish thee peace in all thy ways,
Nor lazy nor contentious days;
And when thy soul and body part,
As innocent as now thou art.
Bishop Richard Corbet

THE BUMBLEBEE

You better not fool with a Bumblebee!—
Ef you don't think they can sting—you'll see!
They're lazy to look at, an' kindo' go
Buzzin' an' bummin' aroun' so slow,
An' ac' so slouchy an' all fagged out,
Danglin' their legs as they drone about
The hollyhawks 'at they can't climb in
'Ithout ist a-tumble-un out agin!
Wunst I watched one climb clean 'way
In a jim'son-blossom, I did, one day,—
An' I ist grabbed it—an' nen let go—
An' *"Ooh-ooh! Honey! I told ye so!"*
Says The Raggedy Man; an' he ist run
An' pullt out the stinger, an' don't laugh none,
An' says: "They *has* ben folks, I guess,
'At thought I wuz predjudust, more er less,—
Yit I still muntain 'at a Bumblebee
Wears out his welcome too quick fer me!"

James Whitcomb Riley

A MAN OF WORDS

A man of words and not of deeds
Is like a garden full of weeds.
When the weeds begin to grow,
It's like a garden full of snow;
When the snow begins to fall,
It's like a bird upon the wall;
When the bird begins to fly,
It's like an eagle in the sky;
When the sky begins to roar,
It's like a lion at the door;
When the door begins to crack,
It's like a whip across your back;

When your back begins to smart,
It's like a penknife in your heart;
And when your heart begins to bleed,
You're dead, you're dead, you're dead indeed.

Anonymous

THE SILVER SWAN

The silver swan, who living had no note,
When death approached, unlocked her silent throat,
Leaning her breast against the reedy shore,
Thus sung her first and last, and sung no more:
Farewell all joys! O death, come close mine eyes;
More geese than swans now live, more fools than wise.

Anonymous

THE BOUNTY OF OUR AGE

To see a strange outlandish fowl,
A quaint baboon, an ape, an owl
A dancing bear, a giant's bone,
A foolish engine move alone,
A morris dance, a puppet-play,
Mad Tom to sing a roundelay,
A woman dancing on a rope,
Bull-baiting also at the *Hope*,
A rhymer's jests, a juggler's cheats,
A tumbler showing cunning feats,
Or players acting on the stage,—
There goes the bounty of our age:
But unto any pious motion
There's little coin and less devotion.

Henry Farley

RELIANCE

Not to the swift, the race:
Not to the strong, the fight:
Not to the righteous, perfect grace:
Not to the wise, the light.

But often faltering feet
Come surest to the goal;
And they who walk in darkness meet
The sunrise of the soul.

A thousand times by night
The Syrian hosts have died;
A thousand times the vanquished right
Hath risen, glorified.

The truth the wise men sought
Was spoken by a child;
The alabaster box was brought
In trembling hands defiled.

Not from my torch, the gleam,
But from the stars above:
Not from my heart, life's crystal stream,
But from the depths of Love.

Henry van Dyke

TO A CHILD

Small service is true service while it lasts:
Of humblest Friends, bright Creature! scorn not one:
The Daisy, by the shadow that it casts,
Protects the lingering dew-drop from the Sun.

William Wordsworth

TRY, TRY AGAIN

'Tis a lesson you should heed,
    Try, try again;
If at first you don't succeed,
    Try, try again;
Then your courage should appear,
For, if you will persevere,
You will conquer, never fear;
    Try, try again.

Once or twice though you should fail,
    Try, try again;
If you would at last prevail,
    Try, try again;
If we strive, 'tis no disgrace
Though we do not win the race;
What should you do in the case?
    Try, try again.

If you find your task is hard,
    Try, try again;
Time will bring you your reward,
    Try, try again.
All that other folks can do,
Why, with patience, should not you?
Only keep this rule in view:
    Try, try again.

T. H. Palmer

Songs Without Music

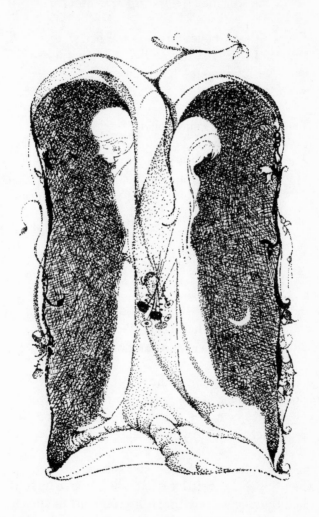

WHEN DAFFODILS

When daffodils begin to peer,
   With heigh! the doxy, over the dale,
Why, then comes in the sweet o' the year;
   For the red blood reigns in the winter's pale.

The white sheet bleaching on the hedge,
   With heigh! the sweet birds, O, how they sing
Doth set my pugging tooth on edge,
   For a quart of ale is a dish for a king.

The lark, that tirra-lirra chants,
   With heigh! with heigh! the thrush and the jay,
Are summer songs for me and my aunts,
   While we lie tumbling in the hay.

William Shakespeare

OH SEND TO ME

Oh send to me an apple that hasn't any kernel,
And send to me a capon without a bone or feather,
And send to me a ring that has no twist or circlet,
And send to me a baby that's all grace and good temper.

How could there be an apple that hasn't any kernel?
How could there be a capon without a bone or feather?
How could there be a ring that has no twist or circlet?
How could there be a baby that's all grace and good temper?

The apple in its blossom hadn't any kernel;
And when the hen was sitting there was no bone or feather;
And when the ring was melting it had no twist or circlet;
And when we were in love there was grace and good temper.

Anonymous

MY HEART'S IN THE HIGHLANDS

My heart's in the Highlands, my heart is not here;
My heart's in the Highlands a-chasing the deer;
Chasing the wild deer, and following the roe,
My heart's in the Highlands wherever I go.
Farewell to the Highlands, farewell to the North,
The birthplace of valor, the country of worth;
Wherever I wander, wherever I rove,
The hills of the Highlands for ever I love.

Farewell to the mountains high covered with snow;
Farewell to the straths and green valleys below;
Farewell to the forests and wild hanging woods;
Farewell to the torrents and loud-pouring floods.
My heart's in the Highlands, my heart is not here,
My heart's in the Highlands a-chasing the deer;
Chasing the wild deer, and following the roe,
My heart's in the Highlands wherever I go.

Robert Burns

HIEMS

When icicles hang by the wall,
  And Dick the shepherd blows his nail,
And Tom bears logs into the hall,
  And milk comes frozen home in pail;
When blood is nipped, and ways be foul,
Then nightly sings the staring owl.
Tu-whit, tu-who! a merry note,
While greasy Joan doth keel the pot.

When all aloud the wind doth blow,
  And coughing drowns the parson's saw,
And birds sit brooding in the snow,

And Marian's nose looks red and raw,
When roasted crabs hiss in the bowl,
Then nightly sings the staring owl,
Tu-whit, tu-who! a merry note,
While greasy Joan doth keel the pot.

William Shakespeare

SPRING

Sound the Flute!
Now it's mute.
Birds delight
Day and Night;
Nightingale
In the dale,
Lark in Sky,
Merrily,
Merrily, Merrily, to welcome in the Year.

Little Boy,
Full of joy;
Little Girl,
Sweet and small;
Cock does crow,
So do you;
Merry voice,
Infant noise,
Merrily, Merrily, to welcome in the Year.

Little Lamb,
Here I am;
Come and lick
My white neck;
Let me pull
Your soft Wool;

Let me kiss
Your soft face:
Merrily, Merrily, we welcome in the Year.
William Blake

MY MOTHER SAID

My Mother said that I never should
Play with the gypsies in the wood,
The wood was dark; the grass was green;
In came Sally with a tambourine.

I went to the sea—no ship to get across;
I paid ten shillings for a blind white horse;
I up on his back and was off in a crack,
Sally tell my Mother I shall never come back.
Anonymous

ARIEL'S SONG

Come unto these yellow sands,
    And then take hands;
Curtsied when you have, and kissed
    The wild waves whist,
Foot it featly here and there;
And, sweet sprites, the burden bear.
    Hark, hark!
        Bow, wow
    The watch-dog bark,
        Bow, wow,
    Hark, hark! I hear
The strain of strutting Chanticleer
Cry, Cock-a-diddle-dow.
William Shakespeare

MY COUSIN GERMAN

My Cousin German came from France
To learn me the Polka dance.
First the heels and then the toes,
That's the way the Polka goes.

Anonymous

THE LAMB

Little Lamb, who made thee,
Dost thou know who made thee,
Gave thee life and bade thee feed
By the stream and o'er the mead;
Gave thee clothing of delight,
Softest clothing, woolly, bright;

Gave thee such a tender voice,
Making all the vales rejoice?
Little Lamb, who made thee?
Dost thou know who made thee?

Little Lamb, I'll tell thee;
Little Lamb, I'll tell thee:
He is callèd by thy name,
For He calls Himself a Lamb.
He is meek, and He is mild,
He became a little child.
I a child and thou a lamb,
We are callèd by His name.
Little Lamb, God bless thee!
Little Lamb, God bless thee!

William Blake

PROUD MAISIE

Proud Maisie is in the wood,
    Walking so early;
Sweet Robin sits on the bush,
    Singing so rarely.

'Tell me, thou bonny bird,
    When shall I marry me?'
'When six braw gentlemen
    Kirkward shall carry ye.'

'Who makes the bridal bed,
    Birdie, say truly?'
'The grey-headed sexton
    That delves the grave duly.

The glow-worm o'er grave and stone
    Shall light thee steady
The owl from the steeple sing,
    "Welcome, proud lady".'

                Sir Walter Scott

THERE WAS A PRESBYTERIAN CAT

There was a Presbyterian cat
Went forth to catch her prey;
She brought a mouse intill the house,
Upon the Sabbath day.
The minister, offended
With such an act profane,
Laid down his book, the cat he took,
And bound her with a chain.

Thou vile malicious creature,
Thou murderer, said he,
Oh do you think to bring Hell
My holy wife and me?
But be thou well assured,
That blood for blood shall pay,
For taking of the mouse's life
Upon the Sabbath Day.

Then he took doun his Bible,
And fervently he prayed,
That the great sin the cat had done
Might not on him be laid.
Then forth to exe-cu-ti-on,
Poor Baudrons she was drawn,
And on a tree they hanged her hie,
And then they sung a psalm.

Anonymous

MUSIC

Orpheus with his lute made trees,
    And the mountain-tops that freeze,
Bow themselves when he did sing.
    To his music plants and flowers
Ever sprung: as sun and showers
    There had made a lasting spring.
Everything that heard him play,
    Even the billows of the sea,
Hung their heads, and then lay by.
    In sweet music is such art,
Killing care and grief of heart
    Fall asleep, or, hearing, die.

John Fletcher

THE SPLENDOR FALLS

The splendor falls on castle walls
   and snowy summits old in story:
The long light shakes across the lakes,
   And the wild cataract leaps in glory,
Blow, bugle, blow, set the wild echoes flying,
Blow, bugle; answer, echoes, dying, dying, dying.

O hark. O hear! how thin and clear,
   And thinner, clearer, farther going!
O sweet and far from cliff and scar
   The horns of Elfland faintly blowing!
Blow, let us hear the purple glens replying:
Blow, bugle; answer, echoes, dying, dying, dying.

O love, they die in yon rich sky,
   They faint on hill or field or river:
Our echoes roll from soul to soul,
   And grow for ever and for ever.
Blow, bugle, blow, set the wild echoes flying,
And answer, echoes, answer, dying, dying, dying.

Lord Tennyson

SONG FOR A DANCE

Shake off your heavy trance!
   And leap into a dance
Such as no mortals use to tread:
   Fit only for Apollo
To play to, for the moon to lead,
   And all the stars to follow!

Francis Beaumont

WHEN AS THE RYE

When as the rye reach to the chin,
  And chopcherry, chopcherry ripe within,
Strawberries swimming in the cream,
And school-boys playing in the stream;
    Then O, then O, then O my true love said,
      Till that time come again,
    She could not live a maid.

George Peele

FROM 'LOVE'S LABOR'S LOST'
(ACT V. SCENE 2)

When icicles hang by the wall,
  And Dick the shepherd blows his nail,
And Tom bears logs into the hall,
  And milk comes frozen home in pail,
When blood is nipp'd, and ways be foul,
Then nightly sings the staring owl,
        Tu-who;
Tu-whit, tu-who—a merry note,
While greasy Joan doth keel the pot.

When all aloud the wind doth blow,
  And coughing drowns the parson's saw,
And birds sit brooding in the snow,
  And Marian's nose looks red and raw,
When roasted crabs hiss in the bowl,
Then nightly sings the staring owl,
        Tu-who;
Tu-whit, tu-who,—a merry note,
While greasy Joan doth keel the pot.

William Shakespeare

THE GOD OF SHEEP

All ye woods, and trees, and bowers,
All ye virtues and ye powers
That inhabit in the lakes,
In the pleasant springs or brakes,
  Move your feet
   To our sound,
  Whilst we greet
   All this ground
With his honor and his name
That defends our flocks from blame.
He is great, and he is just,
He is ever good, and must
Thus be honored. Daffadillies,
Roses, pinks and lovèd lilies
  Let us fling,
  Whilst we sing,
  Ever holy,
  Ever holy,
Ever honored, ever young!
Thus great Pan is ever sung.
      John Fletcher

O, MY LUVE IS LIKE A RED, RED ROSE

O, my luve is like a red, red rose
   That's newly sprung in June:
O, my luve is like the melodie
   That's sweetly played in tune.

As fair art thou, my bonnie lass,
   So deep in luve am I;
And I will luve thee still, my dear,
   Till a' the seas gang dry.

Till a' the seas dang dry, my dear,
   And the rocks melt wi' the sun:
And I will luve thee still, my dear,
   While the sands o' life shall run.

And fare thee weel, my only luve,
   And fare thee weel a while!
And I will come again, my luve,
   Tho' it were ten thousand mile!
              Robert Burns

PIPPA'S SONG
(From *Pippa Passes*)

The year's at the spring
And day's at the morn;
Morning's at seven;
The hill-side's dew -pearled;
The lark's on the wing;
The snail's on the thorn:
God's in His heaven—
All's right with the world!
            Robert Browning

CRADLE SONG

Hush-a-bye, baby, on the tree top,
When the wind blows the cradle will rock;
When the bough breaks the cradle will fall,
Down will come baby and cradle and all.

Anonymous

THE STAR

Twinkle, twinkle, little star,
How I wonder what you are!
Up above the world, so high,
Like a diamond in the sky.

When the blazing sun is gone,
When he nothing shines upon,
Then you show your little light,
Twinkle, twinkle, all the night.

Then the traveller in the dark,
Thanks you for your tiny spark!
He could not see which way to go,
If you did not twinkle so.

In the dark blue sky you keep,
And often through my curtains peep,
For you never shut your eye
Till the sun is in the sky.

As your bright and tiny spark
Lights the traveller in the dark,
Though I know not what you are,
Twinkle, twinkle, little star.

Jane Taylor

JOG ON

Jog on, jog on, the footpath way,
    And merrily hent the stile-a;
A merry heart goes all the day,
    Your sad tires in a mile-a.
                        William Shakespeare

THE SHEPHERD TO HIS LOVE

Come live with me, and be my love,
And we will all the pleasures prove,
That hills and valleys, dales and fields,
Woods or steepy mountain yields.

And we will sit upon the rocks,
Seeing the shepherds feed their flocks
By shallow rivers, to whose falls
Melodious birds sing madrigals.

And I will make thee beds of roses,
And a thousand fragrant posies;
A cap of flowers, and a kirtle,
Embroider'd all with leaves of myrtle;

A gown made of the finest wool,
Which from our pretty lambs we pull;
Fair-linèd slippers for the cold,
With buckles of the purest gold;

A belt of straw and ivy-buds,
With coral clasps and amber studs:
And if these pleasures may thee move,
Come live with me, and be my love.

Thy silver dishes, for thy meat,
As precious as the gods do eat,
Shall on an ivory table be
Prepared each day for thee and me.

The shepherd-swains shall dance and sing
For thy delight each May morning:
If these delights thy mind may move,
Then live with me, and be my love.

Christopher Marlowe

FROM 'A MIDSUMMER-NIGHT'S DREAM'
(ACT II. SCENE 2)

You spotted snakes with double tongue,
   Thorny hedgehogs, be not seen;
Newts and blind-worms, do no wrong,
   Come not near our fairy Queen!

Philomel, with melody
   Sing in our sweet lullaby;
Lulla, lulla, lullaby; lulla, lulla, lullaby;

Never harm, nor spell nor charm,
Come our lovely lady nigh;
So, good-night, with lullaby.

Weaving spiders, come not here;
   Hence, you long-legg'd spinners, hence!
Beetles black, approach not near;
   Worm nor snail, do no offense.

Philomel, with melody
Sing in our sweet lullaby;
Lulla, lulla, lullaby; lulla, lulla, lullaby;
Never harm, nor spell nor charm,
Come our lovely lady nigh;
So, good-night, with lullaby.

William Shakespeare

PIPING DOWN THE VALLEYS WILD

Piping down the valleys wild,
Piping songs of pleasant glee,
On a cloud I saw a child,
And he laughing said to me:

'Pipe a song about a Lamb!'
So I piped with merry chear.
'Piper, pipe that song again;'
So I piped: he wept to hear.

'Drop thy pipe, thy happy pipe;
'Sing thy songs of happy chear:'
So I sung the same again,
While he wept with joy to hear.

'Piper, sit thee down and write
'In a book, that all may read.'
So he vanish'd from my sight,
And I pluck'd a hollow reed,

And I made a rural pen,
And I stain'd the water clear,
And I wrote my happy songs
Every child may joy to hear.

William Blake

FROM 'AS YOU LIKE IT'
(ACT II. SCENE 5)

Under the greenwood tree,
Who loves to lie with me,
And turn his merry note
Unto the sweet bird's throat,
Come hither, come hither, come hither:
Here shall he see no enemy,
But Winter and rough weather.

Who doth ambition shun,
And loves to live i' the sun,
Seeking the food he eats,
And pleased with what he gets,
Come hither, come hither, come hither:
Here shall he see no enemy,
But Winter and rough weather.

William Shakespeare

FULL FATHOM FIVE

Full fathom five thy father lies;
Of his bones are coral made;
Those are pearls that were his eyes:
Nothing of him that doth fade,
But doth suffer a sea-change
Into something rich and strange:
Sea nymphs hourly ring his knell.
Ding-dong!
Hark! now I hear them,
Ding-dong, bell!

William Shakespeare

THE TIGER

Tiger, tiger, burning bright
In the forests of the night,
What immortal hand or eye
Could frame thy fearful symmetry?

In what distant deeps or skies
Burnt the fire of thine eyes?
On what wings dare he aspire?
What the hand dare seize the fire?

And what shoulder and what art,
Could twist the sinews of thy heart?
And when thy heart began to beat,
What dread hand, and what dread feet?

What the hammer? what the chain?
In what furnace was thy brain?
What the anvil? what dread grasp
Dares its deadly terrors clasp?

When the stars threw down their spears,
And watered heaven with their tears,
Did He smile His work to see?
Did He who made the lamb make thee?

Tiger, tiger, burning bright
In the forests of the night,
What immortal hand or eye
Dare frame thy fearful symmetry?

William Blake

LOVE OF FATHERLAND
(From *The Lay of the Last Minstrel*)

Breathes there the man, with soul so dead,
Who never to himself hath said,
   This is my own, my native land!
Whose heart hath ne'er within him burn'd,
As home his footsteps he hath turn'd,
   From wandering on a foreign strand!
If such there breathe, go, mark him well;
For him no Minstrel raptures swell;
High though his titles, proud his name,
Boundless his wealth as wish can claim;
Despite those titles, power, and pelf,
The wretch, concentred all in self,
Living, shall forfeit fair renown,
And, doubly dying, shall go down
To the vile dust, from whence he sprung,
Unwept, unhonor'd, and unsung.

O Caledonia! stern and wild,
Meet nurse for a poetic child!
Land of brown heath and shaggy wood,
Land of the mountain and the flood,
Land of my sires! what mortal hand
Can e'er untie the filial band,
That knits me to thy rugged strand!
                Sir Walter Scott